CRUCIFIED

By

CHRISTIANS

Gene Edwards

The SeedSowers

Crucified by Christians
by
Gene Edwards

Copyright by
Gene Edwards
MCMXCIV

Printed in
the United States of America

Published by
The SeedSowers
P.O. Box 285
Sargent, GA 30275

ISBN 0-940232-52-9
Library of Congress Catalog Card Number: 94-69042

DEDICATION

To

Joe Punzalan

to whom the Lord has given
one of His highest and most
royal of gifts, the gift
of servanthood.

PROLOGUE

PROLOGUE

Thank you for meeting me here at the theatre in such unusual circumstances.

We will find the doors to the theatre open but, strangely enough, most of *the players* are not here tonight. There will be but two actors on stage, and only the two of us in the audience. Ours was a very special invitation to this performance.

Here are our seats. As you can see, we compose the entire audience.

And the stage. How unusual a setting; there is no scenery. An actor sits near the center of the stage, but the lighting has been turned in such a way that no matter the direction we view him, we are never able to clearly see his face.

Ah, there is the second actor. I am impressed to believe that someone feels rather strongly that you and I are in need of being here, and that it is of no small import that we hear what is about to be said.

A production with a title such as this could certainly cause one to pause for reflection, could it not?

Ah, the lights are dimming, the first player is about to address the second.

Act I

1

Welcome, please come in. I've been looking forward to your arrival.

Thank you.

Please take this chair.

I have come here because...because... I am one of those Christians who have been grievously mistreated by other believers. I have found it very difficult to deal with this, and even more difficult to fully recover. I am here in search of help that might lead to my complete healing.

Shattering is it not? Perhaps one of the greatest shocks a Christian will ever know is to discover that fellow Christians can be cruel. Nonetheless, though it seems to be a fact, it is not well known, nor easily accepted.

The discovery that Christians can be cruel to Christians has destroyed the spiritual part of many a believer's

11

life. Few things, even the loss of a loved one, affect one's life so profoundly or so painfully. The damage is quite often unfathomable. I would dare say that a truly vicious attack on the part of one believer to another leaves most Christians so hurt they never fully recover.

Yet, full recovery is possible.

It is good that you have come. Let us trust that you will be one of those who does recover. And fully so. Even *more* than recover.

Have there been many others who have been mis-treated so severely?

A good question. Yes, mistreated, abused—so severely that it amounts to a crucifixion. Sometimes even a public crucifixion.

There were John Huss, Latimer, Tyndale, Wycliff, the maiden Joan, John of Prague...ah, the list seems to be quite large.

But the list is largest in your day; it seems there are many such goings on in your time. Nevertheless, the pattern has been pretty consistent, dating all the way back to, well, the cousin of Jesus.

I have observed that in all these crucifixions each person feels that few others have been so unjustly treated.

2

Has it happened to you?

May I respond to your question by requesting that I lay aside the answer until the close of my time with you. Instead, let us continue pursuing this matter of the devastation a Christian undergoes as a result of being horribly treated by another believer.

As I said, being crucified by fellow Christians is one of the deepest pains a child of God will ever know. It can so profoundly affect you that it can mark the end of your life as a practicing Christian. There is no limit to the effect a crucifixion can have on your life. It could possibly leave you lame for the rest of your life, its destructive power following you throughout your life and on to your grave. On the other hand, it *can* affect you positively—so positively that when you re-emerge, you are almost a totally different person.

I have noted that a crucifixion among ministers can destroy not only the man but his ministry, in totality. Many a servant of God has seen his reputation destroyed, with the event following him all his life, altering not only his life but forever limiting his ministry. Sadly for some, it destroys everything. Of course such wreckage is not confined to ministers as this can be the lot of any believer.

This can be said with certainty: Whether the end result is positive or negative, either way, the destruction is awesome. No one has been adequately prepared for the ordeal of a crucifixion.

But the main question you have to deal with has to do with healing, does it not? The matter of *your* full restitution from out of a deep, deep hurt.

Strangely enough it is not the actual crucifixion that causes the greatest destruction. It is the *aftermath* which devastates even more. Mark my words, for all who have been crucified, there is an aftermath!

You are presently in that very aftermath. Where, then, do you go for that needed healing? Where lies the first step?

The answer is a rather remarkable one.

3

Your first step to recovery? Is it to deal with that person who is most responsible for your being crucified? Do you know this person's name? (Or was it a group of people?) Lay aside his name. The villain lies elsewhere.

Drop the obvious. Place your crucifixion in the realm of the invisibles, in realms unseen. Only there will you truly find the person who deliberately caused you to be crucified. Be assured, this one is not of this earth. Only in the realm of the spirituals will you find the perpetrator. The person who authored the destruction which fell on you, and those inescapable memories of the ghastly deed which now haunt you, began it all in that other realm. It is *outside* of the names of earthly men that you discover your crucifier.

Find him. It is also *there* that you will move toward being healed of those unhealing wounds.

Who is this enemy of yours? Who has wished this ultimate calamity upon your life? He is formidable. Just how formidable? *All* Christians who have ever been crucified have been crucified by *this* one. All. By him and by *no* other.

Can you discover this culprit? Not when you are in as much pain as you have been. Even the wisest of Christians find it difficult to clearly identify the one who *really* caused an unsparing cross.

One thing is sure, the mastermind behind your crucifixion is not one who quickly comes to mind.

May I suggest that there is someone you can speak to about this mystery. He can very quickly identify the one who was behind your crucifixion.

Surely you know the one to ask.

Ask the Crucified One. He knows.

4

Come, stand in the heavenlies, beside your Lord, and see your crucifixion from *His* view. While there, you will come to realize there has never been but one who crucifies, and only one who has been crucified.

Only one?

Yes, only one. When you were crucified at the hands of men, in reality you but entered into *His* crucifixion.

Consider the circumstance which led to His crucifixion. Who caused His cross, His crucifixion? Who was it that plotted His Golgotha? It was exactly the same person who plotted yours. That person actually desired that you enter into your Lord's sufferings. In recent days you have but partaken of *His* loathsome experience. After all, you—the believer—are *in* Him.

Who, then, purposed that the Crucified One be crucified? (And you likewise?) Who caused Jesus to be placed on trial? Who arranged the false witnesses? Who selected the men who would scourge His back and leave it a river of blood? Who selected those who would drive nails into His hands? Who saw to it that there would be so much pain, so much ignominy?

The answer? The same one who caused you to pass through similar circumstances!

A power not known to earth made certain the wood was hewn, the cross fashioned and then lifted up, the spear at hand.

Who crucified you? The same one who crucified your Lord. Inquire of Him as to who authored His crucifixion.

Do you hear His response?
Who crucified Me?
Who planned My crucifixion?
My Father.
It was My Father.

Hard words to hear, yes. Nor is it easy to reconcile such incongruity.

Nonetheless, the Father willed His own Son's crucifixion. And yours. The plan and the executing of that plan was His. He even made sure it would be at the hands of Christians, just as it was the Lord's very own people who crucified Him. A double pain!

Come to grips with this, that your Father—and your Lord's Father—willed that you be crucified. Accepting this terrible but immovable fact is *your* first step to healing. Take that step and recovery begins. Failing that, nothing else will ever work to your complete restoration. Healing is embedded in the act of your turning to your Lord and accepting this terrible tragedy as having come from *His* hand. Bitter, yes. Incomprehensible, yes. Embrace it you must. For essential it is.

If you refuse?

Hear my words. Refusal to accept your crucifixion as wholly from the hand of God only means you were not crucified, you were just mistreated. Only when you accept that it came from God...only then is it a *true* crucifixion. The crucifixion of a Christian comes from the hand of God, and God alone.

5

Among believers a true crucifixion has but one author. He writes the script for all.

Just how involved is your Lord in a crucifixion? In yours? He arranges every detail.

He not only writes the script, He, and He alone, selects the participants. He choreographs every detail, in every scene. He is in charge of the lighting. He selects the stage. He creates the sets, the scenery. He chooses the bit actors, walk-ons and extras. He even selects the audience... those who view your crucifixion.

He selected the ones who bore false witness against you; those who would spread the rumors, those who whispered behind your back. He chose those who finally called you forth for trial. He scripted the harsh words hurled at you. He cast the one who hurled those words. He knew which of those words would crush you and ring in your ears for years to come.

They do still burn as fire in your soul, do they not? Even now they echo across the chambers of your memory, is that not true?

Your Father also ordained the results of the crucifixion. The very *process* of crucifixion was His to direct, selecting even the ones who smashed the nails into your wrists and rammed that still-felt spear into your side. He knew your heart would be broken and how much torment your soul would suffer.

From those who are most involved, right on down to the casual passers-by, *your Lord* is the author of the script, the casting director and, most of all, the producer.

Every crucifixion contains certain characteristics common to all crucifixions: Rejection. Pain. Unfairness. Rumor. Innuendoes. More pain. Misunderstanding. Demeaning. Belittling. Loss of reputation. Loss of friends. Often, there is excommunication. The loss of *all* things.

In it all, come to know this, it was your Father's will for you to taste all these things!!

Most of all, the God and Father of the Lord Jesus Christ deliberately, with forethought, with studied reason, selected the one who was to be crucified! The characters, the places of crucifixion, the words to be spoken, yes. All that. Then He selected the *victim*.

From out of the crowd, He selected *you*!

You! To be so brutally, viciously, heartlessly, publicly, ignominiously crushed. You, to become a spectacle in the sight of men and angels.

There is only one conclusion that you, as a believer, can come to: that you were *honored*!!

Now, can you lay hold of a way to survive so great an honor!?

6

An honor? That? An honor!

This simply cannot be, can it? Such a thought flies in the face of all human reason, does it not?

But you have no idea what was said to me, said of me, and done to me. It was vicious. Inhumane...beyond words. Unjust. Unfair beyond belief. God would never have authored so heartless a deed as was my ordeal! Would He?

Yes, He would. Remember, He has already done this *at least once* before!

Pause and consider that there was once a crucifixion far, far more unjust, more brutal than yours. Yet your Father planned every moment of it. He even planned it before the foundation of creation...the crucifixion of His only Son.

Such thought is really not all that inconceivable after all, is it? He moved the circumstances of heaven and earth

25

to see that this horrid event took place exactly as He planned.

Be driven to this simple fact; you must find a whole new view of your crucifixion. There was far more purpose in it than you first realized; is this not true? Perhaps far more good in its content than you can presently imagine.

But! You must yield to the author!

Can you see your Lord as the perpetrator of your crucifixion? If so, peace will not be far behind. Look up! Behold your crucifixion. It was not yours at all, but the crucifixion of your Lord. His agony and death took place on a far higher plane than mortal eye could see on that dark day, or on any day since.

What happened to you was meant to be a magnificent beginning of transformation in your life. The circumstances which birthed this tragedy were exactly what you needed. That hellish event brought you to exactly the place your Lord wants you to be.

It was an act of love. Accept that fact; then will that day cease to be an ugly, nightmarish scene, the memory of which will otherwise never let you go.

Make this your prayer: "A sovereign act, my God, pouring forth out of the fountain of your mercy."

Destruction, an act of love? A demonstration of mercy?

Yes! See that... and embrace it!

It is, as I said, an honor to be selected by your Lord to be crucified, but only as you do honor to His sovereign hand.

> *Lord, the circumstances leading to my crucifixion were yours. They came not from men, as first I had thought. Father, I accept it all. All...as coming from you.*

7

But why me? Why something as extreme as a crucifix-
ion? What good is there in it? Why my crucifixion? Why
me, of all people; and why at the hands of Christians?

The answer is found in the purpose of any crucifixion.
There is but one purpose: to destroy! The cross destroys
in the most destructive way possible. A crucifixion is
nothing less than destruction to the uttermost, destruction
so vast only divinity could be its author.

The false witness against you, the verdict, the nails,
the cast spear, all had a singular purpose—your destruction.

One who has passed through such a crucible need not
be told that it pushes the soul to the edge of spiritual
oblivion.

There are two kinds of destruction, though. Only one
leads upward. The other is like a rock smashed against the
face of a clock: Your Christian life does not move forward

from that day. The destruction is even compounded if you chew on the horrid memory of the deed, if you continually relive the hurt and anger. That is one way a crucifixion destroys a Christian. Do you wish to live in such a state?

In another realm, through other eyes, and with a wholly different set of values, one sees a wholly different state of destruction.

God desires to forever destroy certain elements in your makeup. This is intended for good! It is for you, then, to see these events on a far deeper level.

The inherent nature of a crucifixion is destructive. This is the key to understanding your crucifixion. In that discovery you may also find healing... and recovery. Perhaps you will even lay hold of a higher plane of living. But be warned, if you choose the more surface view of the destructive nature of the cross, then the hands on that clock never move again.

8

Did you not once tell your Lord that you wished to be His?

Did you not say to Him that you agreed to allow into your life whatever He willed . . . that He could do anything in order to bring about your transformation? Remember that moment when you asked to be conformed to His image? Consider this: Transformation hinges on your becoming a living sacrifice.

The only other road is self-protection.

His will in your life almost always includes a very memorable hour of virtually total destruction!

Your destruction. Your death.

But remember, it is your death being brought about in a manner similar to His death. Destruction is what *He* experienced on the cross. It was a divine destruction, one that fell out to the accomplishment of divine purpose.

Never forget, your Lord was destroyed! Publicly. Brutally.

Oh, but He rose from the dead!

True. Consider now the implication of that very fact... as it relates to you.

The negative aspects of your being would be hit very hard by a crucifixion, would they not? Be assured, the dark side of your nature does react very harshly to being crucified. The dark side of a person does not want to be crucified. It does not even want to be *criticized*. Our dark side never wants to be dealt with, not on any level. When you are being crucified, your dark side emerges in full fury and in clear focus. It becomes extremely visible and clearly exposed!

Who you really are is starkly revealed during a crucifixion.

Only a crucifixion, a very unfair crucifixion, can accomplish this unveiling.

Can you, then, see His hand in all this?

If there is darkness to be brought to light, hidden motives to be exposed, weaknesses to be found, surely they emerge into the light in the agonies of being crucified.

There is nothing which more exposes a Christian's weakness than *how he reacts* to being crucified by other Christians. Whole worlds of things about *you* are brought to light when you are crucified.

Unfortunately, some refuse to go to the cross, but resist most adamantly.

Which brings us to a central question.

How did you handle being crucified by other Christians?

9

Was there anger? Resentment? Attack? What was your conduct? Did you find fault? Did you analyze others' actions, even scrutinizing their smallest deed and motive? In other words, did your dark side emerge? Your answer may again shed light on the purpose of God in allowing you to pass through these waters.

How did you do?

You need not reply if your answer is embarrassing, and it probably is. You can be comforted that most believers do not do very well at being crucified. Their usual conduct? Typically, Christians resent. They argue. They defend. They attack. They reason. They talk—a great deal! They internalize. Most nurture a grudge and keep kindled a fire of the horrible memories. (Generally speaking, Christians are not very Christian when they are crucified.)

Do you recall such reactions on your part?

If so, consider this: God may wish to bring you beyond all such reactions.

The question really is central, then, is it not? What was your conduct? Whatever your reactions were to a crucifixion, consider them.

Find solace in this: In all Christian history believers who handle a crucifixion nobly are virtually unknown.

Perhaps there have never been any who have handled a crucifixion perfectly. A few have handled theirs brilliantly, but even here most of these believers were crucified at the hands of heathen, not Christians. Being brutally treated by fellow Christians puts one in a situation far more difficult to handle.

Crucifixion, taken at the highest level, is contrary to everything that is human nature. Each believer, to see events as the eyes of God sees them, must step beyond reason, and certainly beyond logic.

This means you must step beyond your opinion of what God is like. Step, now, into a realm which has a value system at war with yours.

You like your God when He lets you have a nice home, a good car and good circumstances, do you not? When He lets you sell your house and buy another one? When you get that scholarship, procure that job? But what is your attitude toward Him when that same Lord gives consent to nails tearing through your flesh, ripping your feet, and shredding your soul? Do you still like Him? As much?!

Let this possibility into your heart, that your Lord might want to so order your life that you will learn... *learn*... to like Him no matter what He permits to come into your life.

There is another question which lies just beyond "How did I react to being crucified?" The second question for you to consider is, "Do I wish to go on in my present attitude toward what happened? Shall this be my state?"

Be aware that many Christians choose *not* to be fully restored. Some believers actually prefer being wounded...permanently. You have but two choices, recovery and healing, or your present state.

Be warned, if you are healed, that means you cannot resent anymore. Some believers cannot handle such a thought; they need to go on resenting, arguing and remembering. Shall this be your lot?

It would not be untypical for you to choose to hate rather than to be healed.

A return to innocence! Can that be realized? If so, can you handle it!? If you continue to blame, no. If you continue to relive the memories, no.

But I lost everything in that crucifixion!

So have many others. Lives, ministries, organizations. Churches have been destroyed. Families smashed. Total, utter ruin. That is not the issue.

The issue is: Do you wish to place that crucifixion behind you? Are you willing to see it as a necessary and beautiful experience that was intended to bring you *life* and to bring you light? Or do you prefer to nurse the hurt? Is forever living in its deathly dark shadow your choice?

You...*were*...crucified by plan, by permission and by preference. You were crucified by the will of God.

He alone is the one you make peace with.

Forgiving God is not easy. Seeing no evident reason for all this and, yet, accepting it. Seeing the unseen is not easy...only *necessary*.

10

What will be the result if you embrace a crucifixion?

To embrace it is to allow the destruction of all that is in you which is not Christ. When you embrace a crucifixion, you allow the full element of destruction into your life to do away with the very thing which you so desperately desire to preserve. Crucifixion strikes at the most subterranean motivations of your being, the labyrinth of your unconscious will.

The very desire to not be destroyed must be destroyed. At least that desire shall be dealt a heavy blow. The cross seeks out man's desire to not suffer, and man's furious commitment to never lose, and his screaming logic that he is not in the wrong.

Rumors and innuendoes about your Lord swarmed about everywhere the weekend He was crucified. Some of those rumors still survive and circulate until this very day... and will continue to do so until the end of time.

It will be the same with you. Your repulsion at having to live an entire lifetime with lies will destroy you. Either that, or your repulsion will be destroyed, and replaced with patience and divine acceptance.

Just how adversely has your crucifixion affected your life? Are you fearful of going wholeheartedly after your Lord again? Fearful of trusting other believers? Fearful for, and even cynical of, new believers who are in the first flush of love for their Lord? If so, then the effect has been profound, indeed.

Embrace that cross, and these dark brown attitudes will yield.

Face your own conduct.

Again, I remind you that the dark side of all believers tends to emerge as they pass through the trial, the judgment, the scourging, the nails, the spear, the naked exposure, the jeers.

Among those who crucified you, there might be one who remembers you as one who did a little crucifying of others! Did you? Did you return fire with fire? Were you capable of hate? Or at least, major flares of anger? Did you show it? Did you, too, become unethical? Did you do a bit of defending of yourself? Can you see that even a defensive rebuttal speaks volumes of you? Reflect on this question: Do you count your negative reaction as being a minor thing?

Do you have any idea how much of your dark side dies in an embraced crucifixion?

Probably your crucifiers thought what they did to you was a small thing! They may have thought that it was *your* conduct that was outrageous!

It is not God's intention to allow a crucifixion to become a platform for self-defense. A crucifixion has one purpose, to destroy elements in you which *need* to be crucified.

If you embrace a crucifixion?

You will lose a great number of enemies and a large number of bitter memories. You will also see the death of a portion of your dark side.

11

Wherein lies your disappointment? Where is centered your greatest pain? How tightly do you hold on to that injustice?

A position denied? A title? Something taken from you that you valued? Something you deserved denied you? Something you did not deserve done to you? Position? Recognition? Eldership? Acceptance? Approval? Your way!? Honor never bestowed? Or being lied about?

Crucifixions do two things. They reveal—and they destroy.

Long ago Christians crucified a man by the name of John Huss.

They found charges which they considered to be worthy of an ecclesiastical trial. When the trial began, they did not allow Huss to present any evidence, or even to speak. They refused to read his writings or hear his defense. Now *that* is unjust.

But these injustices did not keep them from taking Huss outside the city of Constance, Germany, tying him to a pole and burning him, and then ordering men to shovel up the dirt around the site (until they had dug a large hole in the ground) and cast the dirt into the river, just to make sure not one of his ashes would remain on earth!

Still, Huss died without ire.

Men honored Joan of Arc in the same way. She accepted her fate and died in quiet praise.

Deacons hated their pastor so much that when they fired him, they would not pay him his last week's salary. When asked why, they responded, "Because we want him to suffer."

That is unjust! But it happens—and it comes from God!!

What is revealed in such hours is the result of a sovereign act of God. What is revealed, if one dares to look, can also be devastating. It is difficult to pause and look, is it not?

But remember, if you continue to nurse the nightmare, you must never think of what happened to you as being crucifixion.

The purpose of a crucifixion is to lay naked before the world, men, God, and angels your reaction to being crucified.

42

A crucifixion reveals one's reaction to being crucified.

If you become angry, fight back, argue, shout or scream, if you accuse and blame... that is where things will stay. Be sure, that is not a crucifixion. That is simply people being vicious to one another.

Is not every crucifixion a real crucifixion? If not, what is a real crucifixion?

A *true* crucifixion has resolution. A true crucifixion ever ends in triumph!

If you accept that nightmarish ordeal as a sovereign work of God, if you acquiesce to His will, then does *He* begin to have His will. Suddenly it becomes not only a crucifixion but a holy work of God. Things needing destruction begin to be destroyed. Things He desires live on... live on *in victory*.

Persist in looking upon that event as the unjustifiable conduct of wicked men and nothing is gained. Its only outcome is a shriveled soul. Your future then becomes no more than that which awaits any embittered creature.

But take heart. Even now it is not too late to allow that event to be taken as wholly from the hand of God. Receive it as being from Him for your good. For your transformation. For the destruction of the dark side of your person. For resurrection.

Act II

12

Come with me to a high hill.

See upon the brow of that hill three men. They are all there being crucified. There is no difference in the manner of their execution (all crucifixions are the same). It is only their reactions which are different.

All three were crucified—brutally. All three were ignominiously crucified. Each showed a different attitude toward crucifixion. Each was different in the way he died. Each man reacted differently to circumstances that were identical. Each reacted differently to those who were crucifying them.

Note how much each man had to say about his crucifixion. Two said much; one said nothing. That fact really does tell you a great deal about each man's attitude toward the cross.

Let us draw closer and learn from each of these three men.

The first person we meet is a convicted thief. We shall call his name Haroc.

Haroc stole for a living and, in so doing, stole one time too often. Caught, tried, sentenced, the punishment decreed was death. Death in the extreme.

From Haroc's view, it was not his first time to be crucified. From his view he had been crucified by other people throughout all his life.

The first time he was ever mistreated he reacted savagely. He remonstrated that he had been terribly and unjustly treated. After that day, when you met him, his main topic of conversation would be recounting how he had been mistreated by others.

At some point in his life it seemed to him that unjust crucifixion came into his life with increased frequency. In the grip of his own attitude Haroc became incapable of seeing anything as his fault. Everything negative which happened to him was both unfair and never his fault.

The first time he was caught stealing, his reaction was predictable. He blamed others.

You might say Haroc was the author of what has become the prevailing view of most people who are crucified: Declare verbal war on those doing the crucifying, protest your innocence, scream the injustice, and point out the minute inconsistencies of the adversary.

On the day Haroc was crucified he made quite a scene of it all. As he blamed others, he made sure he took no responsibility... for anything. His thoughts were focused only on the ones responsible for his plight. Making that point his focus, Haroc missed out on healing, redemption and resurrection. (His was not a wise choice!) Tragic, was it not, with recovery from crucifixion so near. Healing was not only close, that healing had a name. Healing's *name* is Jesus Christ.

While hanging there, Haroc blamed God for his crucifixion. He also blamed men. Haroc covered both possibilities! God and man.

You, too, were either crucified by men or by God. These are your choices. There are no others.

Choose to blame men and your state is hopeless. Choose God and you have found the right person; nonetheless, if you blame Him, your state remains hopeless. Follow either path and you join the ranks of the unhealable.

Haroc had another choice. Not "You, God are to blame; so are the men who have crucified me." But "Lord, you did this for my good and the good of others; get on with it."

Haroc showed no redemptive attitude toward crucifixion. Yet a redemptive attitude is the only *safe* attitude to have, when one is hanging on a cross.

Haroc had missed the true purpose of being crucified.

Odd, is it not, that if you miss the purpose of your crucifixion, you actually miss being crucified! So it was with Haroc. He wasted his crucifixion! He simply received punishment for his deeds.

No man is truly crucified until he accepts that crucifixion as coming from the hand of God. Otherwise, it amounts to no more than an ugly incident taking place between ugly people.

You happen to be a follower of Jesus Christ, are you not? Odd things happen to those who follow Him who is The Crucified One. The very word *crucifixion* implies that you, His follower, are to receive from the hands of others that which is unfair, unjust, undeserved. The word also implies that God is the author of that crucifixion, and hidden in its ordeal is a grand purpose that cannot be visibly seen.

Haroc missed that purpose. There never came that pivotal moment when he yielded up to God the grizzly hour. Consequently, Haroc's crucible was of no benefit to him or to anyone. Haroc spewed bitterness. He fought being crucified. That, dear child of God, is a wasted crucifixion!

Utterly wasted!

I trust yours will not be.

Imagine for a moment what it would have been like if Haroc had been pulled down off his cross before dying. Haroc, *saved from crucifixion*, now there is a thought indeed (and it certainly was Haroc's desire to escape the ordeal).

Is it not true that you, too, wish your crucifixion had never happened? Did you not hope—desperately hope— you could be saved from it midway through its agonies? So it is with all men. After all, by its very nature, a cross *is* unbearable.

But on to the central question. Would anything have changed in Haroc's life if he had escaped his crucifixion the next day? Would there have been gain in his heart and life?

Here is a better question yet: Does escaping a crucifixion ever change us for the better?

The answer must be...no!

What would Haroc's future have been had he slipped past death?

Imagine Haroc walking away from Golgotha! Do you see his life change at all? No. The next day Haroc would have been exactly the man he had previously been. Saving him from crucifixion would not have worked betterment in him. So it is with all men.

Had you been *saved* from the crucifixion you have passed through, it would *not* have made you a better Christian! Being saved from crucifixion at the hands of other Christians does not better any believer spiritually!

Do you wish to continue being the same person you were before you were crucified? If so, you miss God's purpose.

A crucifixion, properly embraced, will ultimately make you far more than what you were. Improperly embraced, it leaves you less than what you were. *It is your choice.* You will either be spiritually destroyed or you will grow in Christ beyond previous boundaries!

Your future holds only two alternatives. You will be better off, or *worse* off. Tell me, up until now, have you gained ground or lost ground? The answer should be so evident it requires no reflection...especially if you have gained ground, for the gain is overwhelming, and wonderful.

The other alternative? Consider Haroc for the source of your answer.

Had Haroc been delivered from his ordeal, and had you met him on the morrow, you would have found him more bitter, more victimized, more *innocent* than before. Be sure, Haroc would have gone out of his way to show you his mutilated hands.

Men come out of a crucifixion far better or far worse.

Men meant it to me for evil.

God meant it to me for evil.

OR ...

God meant it to me for good.

The only possible way a crucifixion could affect Haroc was to change him for the worse. Would you join his tribe?

Again, I inquire, up until now has your crucifixion affected you for the worse? Remember, a crucifixion alters your Christian life forever.

If you are not sure of your answer, it probably means you are worse off. Why? Because, when a crucifixion is received on its highest level, it is never seen as negative.

Contrast what happened in the life of Haroc as over against that of Jesus. One of these two ends must be yours! Which will it be—Haroc's crucifixion, or Jesus'?

Haroc died only a few inches from the very model of *how to be crucified.* So do all men! Alas, Haroc could have even risen from the dead. Wherein was

Haroc's oversight? He blamed. He saw himself as victim. To know true crucifixion, these are two luxuries you cannot afford. If you blame, do you know whom you are ultimately blaming? Ultimately, you blame your Lord. But, oh, if you accept that gory day from Him, then glory awaits!

There is a fine line in a crucifixion: it is a line between disaster and waste, as over against resurrection and glory.

You have been angry. You have blamed. You have been the victim. You have often recalled the event of your victimization. Bitterness is at the door. Continue on this path and you lose all that God is seeking to accomplish in you.

Look up. What happened to you was an act of sovereign mercy.

But Jesus was God! I am at a great disadvantage!

Yes, that is true. But so was the *second* thief! Let us now consider him.

13

We shall call his name Betard.

Betard was crucified at the same time, in the same way as Haroc. Betard *started out* handling his crucifixion the way Haroc did. So do most men!

On the way to being crucified, Betard had but one thought: "How can I get out of this?" Having failed at escaping, he argued and blamed, kicked and screamed. When the nails rammed their way through his flesh, Betard bellowed in protest. There was no one within miles of him but what they knew Betard was being crucified.

Though caught in the act of his crime, Betard protected his innocence. When placed in jail, he recounted his story of injustice to anyone who would listen. His defense was logical—so much so that it was not only plausible but irresistible.

Does this sound familiar?

Betard followed a pattern similar to most believers today who are crucified by fellow Christians. (When a Christian is mistreated, he can create quite a scene. He attacks. He tells anyone willing to listen all about every detail of what was so dastardly done to him.)

Betard was not handling his crucifixion, was he? In fact, not one whit better than Haroc.

Betard began his ordeal by calling down curses on his enemies. He cursed his companion, he railed at the watching crowds, cursed the guards. He blamed everyone in sight. Then he turned and ranted at God. At least in doing that, he had found the proper person to blame! Railing at his dying Companion he found his proper target. A bitter old man was coming to his end, expiring in the womb of resentment.

Had Betard been taken down from his cross, would he have been a changed man?

Deliverance from a crucifixion is an escape from pain. It is also an escape from change... change which God desires. If Betard (and you) escaped crucifixion, in the long run would either of you be better off?

Consider this, if today you were to ask Betard that same question, "Would you be better off had you escaped the cross," there is no question but what Betard would tell you that escape from crucifixion would have been the worst thing that could have befallen him.

Today Betard is *glad* he was crucified.

May such a day come to you.

If you wish to receive counsel on escaping crucifixion *never ask Betard*. He will encourage you to yield! Betard

56

knows the redemptive, transformational powers of ignominy.

The best day that thief ever lived was the day he was heartlessly, cruelly, and publicly crucified!

The best day he *ever* lived.

Today, knowing what he knows, Betard would have embraced that cross in a manner that would establish a model for us all.

May the day come when men hear you say "Oh, for the good that came into my life as a result, I would change nothing. I thank God that he allowed me to know such defamation."

Something monumental happened to Betard. He changed his view of the events.

May that happen to you.

If you allow the ill treatment inflicted on you by other believers to solidify into bitterness, you will be as the first thief. But if something turns...

What happened that changed Betard?

He noticed Jesus. He finally saw his Lord.

He watched God crucified. He witnessed a crucifixion, and he saw a proper response to man's inhumanity to man. The third victim, Jesus, had made peace with being crucified. And never forget, He was being crucified by His brethren.

That sight changed the thief. Be wise, emulate him!

Consider Jesus. As you are crucified, watch *Him* handle His crucifixion. Your Lord bequeathed to you an example of the high art of being crucified!

As you consider that incredible scene, know that it is He, and He alone, who knew the cross better than all others, who, nonetheless, chooses *who* will be crucified. The Crucified One chooses *who* it will be that follows Him to Golgotha, there to be crucified even by brethren.

The Crucified One, having tasted the very ends of the ghastliness of the cross, hesitated not one whit to chose you to be crucified. Crucified by an instrument called *Christians*!

If Christ had never been crucified, yet had selected you to be crucified, that would be a different matter. But He *knew* what you would go through!

Betard noticed.

Betard beheld how God handled losing all His friends! Betard watched Jesus' reactions toward everyone. Betard watched God experience failure; he saw God in the act of losing everything. That amazing sight changed Betard.

May it change you.

In that bloody moment Betard saw, and having seen, took action. First he repented   he took responsibility for his deeds. None of us are totally free of the need of doing that, especially if it is friends who set out to crucify you. It is just not possible to be totally perfect in your response to such betrayal.

Secondly, Betard *stopped* his protest. He *forever* shut his mouth. He ended his negations, his protestations Betard stopped referring to being crucified. Forever!

"Hush" was the exact word he used. He called out to his fellow thief. "Silence!" At that moment Betard won!

Perhaps it will be the same for you, when—concerning this matter—silence at last reigns in your inmost being. That is the moment when *all* begins to change. This is the point where a crucifixion begins to accomplish its purpose.

Betard won. He won over his adversaries and his adversities. He won over his anger. He won over his memories! He triumphed over crucifixion.

"Silence!" he cried. "These things are from the hand of God!"

There was the life changer.

There is nothing more wonderful than for a man to gain an instinct about how to be crucified. "Now I see how I am supposed to walk in this hour." Ah, *this* is a crucifixion, a real crucifixion. A *Christian* crucifixion, designed for a Christian. Here is where all of us learn to be Christians!

In these simple elements, presented to you by a thief, you find the proper way to hang on a cross! The way of total healing from all the wounds and pains of the cross come pouring into your heart.

Two men show you how. One is the God-man. The other, a felon.

On that day of ultimate infamy, when Jesus Christ was illegally tried, unjustly sentenced, brutally murdered... many watched. But only one... saw!

May you be the next who sees!

The enemies of Jesus watched in somber satisfaction; His former friends watched in confusion and shame. But of all those who watched Him, there was but one person, only one, who called Him *Lord*.

"Lord," cried the thief! "Lord!" In that moment an ignorant man saw sovereignty. Betard was freed from all the damage of crucifixion! He saw his Sovereign working out his sovereignty. He found expression of divine revelation in one word! "Lord!"

When others are making you a villain, is it not true that everything in you wants to talk about it and, in so doing, justify yourself? Jesus Christ did not justify; He did not defend. He allowed the full brunt of that whole tragedy to whelm Him.

Christ saw *His* Lord, and the thief saw Christ!

"You are behind it all, Lord" was their common ground.

Once the thief saw he was no longer being punished, he was truly being crucified. Nay, he was being *destroyed*. That day, as he embraced crucifixion, the dark side of Betard's nature died. Crucified for *his good*, and for the Lord's glory.

That gory scene on Golgotha suddenly became a very Christian event. The cross had suddenly turned not only into redemption but also transformation!

All crucifixions are intended to turn into redemption and transformation. Crucifixions are *not* for pain nor bitterness, they are for the highest of triumphs.

At that moment there was no thief; there were but two brothers dying together. Betard had entered into the fellowship of the sufferings and crucifixion of his Lord.

Would you not also enter into His suffering? Enter into His cross? Forsake your crucifixion; become part of His! May you have that privilege and joy.

Here is the joy of destruction, and of seeing destruction destroyed. Unfairness turned to transformation. "Crucified by men" changed into triumph by Christ. It is in the joy of that moment, when the smoke and fire lift, you see Jesus!

All this, found in one contrite word, "Lord!"

Betard, in some flash of light sent to him by God, understood the true meaning of crucifixion. He saw the drama going on behind the scenes, in the unseen. Betard learned all this in the face of the *only* person who has ever truly been crucified. Betard had touched resurrection. Even ascension.

You are presently where that thief was that day. You are in the hellish vortex of nightmarish destruction.

Your Lord has arranged at least two crucifixions.

The thief's...and yours!

Be as wise as that thief. Never allow a crucifixion to be from men. Allow it only to be from God.

> *It is from you, my Lord! For my good! This thing is wholly between you and me. There are no others involved in this bloody hour. I do not like this; it is the most difficult thing ever to enter my life. But it is you. I now call you Lord, sovereign Lord. Others meant it to me for evil; Lord, you meant it to me for good! I accept this crucifixion! From you!*

61

Take it at the highest. Clasp the hand of God. Receive this ignominy as glory. Draw it into your very bosom. Draw in the shame. Embrace the pain. Lift the cup high. Lift it to heaven; nay, lift it to Him. Then drink the cup! All of it.

Perhaps you, like so many others, including the thief, did not handle your crucifixion very well, not at the outset. But it is never too late!

Today you can take that crucifixion you perhaps unjustly received . . . take it out of the accident of circumstance, out of the acts of men, out of the hands of Christians, and place it back into the hands of God. May it become a crucifixion which came only from God.

Lord, my life ended with yours on Golgotha.
My life began that day for the same reason.
Nothing less could have saved me, nor worked
so much good and so much life into me.

14

Now we turn to that third man, the Carpenter. He was crucified more brutally and more unfairly than any other Christian! His conduct that day was flawless.

What Jesus felt while being accused, then tried and finally convicted, must have hurt in much the same way you now hurt. That being true, do you realize what a beautiful legacy He left you? He presented you with a treasure: He pioneered for you the way to go through a crucifixion. He cleared a path, showing you not only *how* to go through it, but how to order your life *after* it is over. After all, what happens to a person *after* he is nailed to a cross is often more difficult to deal with than the crucifixion itself. Has that not been true for you? Pause then and consider another legacy He left you, how to order your life in these days *after* your crucifixion.

No one will ever live up to the standard your Lord established that day. Nonetheless, it forever remains your model to behold.

During the trial, the climb to Golgotha, the cross, through it all, He was poetry itself. During those last six hours of His life, He left for every believer a portrait of how to react to even the most extreme injustices.

Behold how He reacted to betrayal, to lies, to false witnesses. These are all instruments men used, and for but one purpose, to inflict pain. Instruments which, in our enlightened age, *Christians* employ when crucifying one of their own. You have tasted these instruments. You have felt the pain they are designed to inflict, these tools which serve as *preludes to crucifixion*.

Jesus Christ absorbed these pains, even as they added the shamefulness of being crucified in public. Humiliated, degraded, defamed, tortured and then murdered.

That day He raised *acceptance* of the cross into an *art form*.

He was the only one not saying ugly things. He alone was allowing the cross to take its course.

He had learned.

What had he learned? To accept *all* things from the hand of His Father.

Others are talking about you, are they not? In so doing they are making you the villain. You want to *do* something about that, do you not? Jesus Christ did not justify. He did not defend. He allowed the full brunt of that entire horror to come to Him.

Hearts wonder and break. Spirits stand in awe. There is no greater evidence of His Godship than that which was seen displayed by Him that day! His relationship to an ignominious crucifixion tells men who He is.

There was no dark side to this one!

But there is more.

His triumph over being crucified holds the key to *your* triumph over the deed perpetrated on you by other believers.

How in?

It is extremely important that you know the answer to that question.

15

This One who died so magnificently lives inside you at this moment.

The Life of God which dwelt in Jesus Christ, the life source which saw Him through those horrible hours, that Life which was in Him, that Life which allowed Him to live above the moment, *that same Life* indwells you today.

Behold the operation of that Life as it worked in Him. Behold the power of an indwelling Lord as the Father worked in the Son in the face of crucifixion. The Lord Jesus, by the power of His Father's indwelling life...

criticized no one,
gave no rebuttal,
never resorted to logic or reason,
did not defend His rights,
gave no defense,
challenged no lies,
answered only with silence.

Magnificent, thunderous *silence*.

What an incredible Life it must have been which indwelt Jesus Christ. Well, dear one, that same Life now indwells you! Touch that Life; let that Life be the power to walk as He walked. That Life is practiced at seeing a believer through the cross.

16

Why did your Lord not answer those who charged Him with villainy? Others do, yet He did not. It was because He understood the fundamental nature of a crucifixion: Those present give no value to your answers. Those present are not there to hear; they are there only to turn your words against you, regardless of what you respond. At the actual time of a crucifixion, all issues are long past the point of reasonableness.

In His case, an answer given would have been heard only by the ears of hate. There is not a sentence in the lexicon of men that would have been accepted that day. His words, had He spoken, would have been twisted and hurled back at him. The simplest utterance would have been seen as irrefutable proof of His guilt. Your Lord could not have spoken an acceptable word that day.

It is perhaps an error in reasoning to believe discussion, facts, logic or Scripture are of any weight at such moments. Recrimination is the order of the day. Hearts are fixed. Punishment is inevitable.

Proof of this state of mind came when, at last, He did speak. How simple can a sentence be? "It is as you say." But to the ears of His enemies that small word was enough to justify crucifying Him.

Learn this well: Defense is useless in a crucifixion. Yet remaining quiet is virtually impossible. Find that Life in you which can provide all you need, in all aspects of the cross. Again, that Life knows how to take you through a crucifixion.

God and angels must have stood in awe of such dignity in the presence of such rejection. Calm. Silent. Thunderously silent. He raised the standard of the conduct of one being victimized to breathtaking new heights.

As exemplary as was His conduct, we should not be too surprised, for He had walked with such bearing throughout His entire life. His every step and every word were but preparation for that dark hour. He had lived His entire life in the shadow of a crucifixion and in preparation for being crucified!

So ought, also, all His followers.

17

To understand fully your Lord's calm and dignity you must grasp what happened the evening before.

The evening *before* Golgotha was every bit as black as His crucifixion. Had it not been for the ministering of an angel that evening, your Lord might have died of sheer agony.

What happened that night? Your Lord faced His Father...in a garden. In that garden He gained the central ingredient necessary to triumph over crucifixion.

If you are to know total healing and total release from the memories, the scars, of your own horrible day, it will be necessary for you to come to this same garden and lay hold of that same ingredient.

What is this which is so crucial? Why is this rendezvous with God so crucial?

I speak of Gethsemane.

A Gethsemane can be as horrible as a crucifixion. You see this fact clearly as you realize your Lord did not easily pass through His Gethsemane. Neither will it be easy for you.

Thank God, there was a moment of yielding in Gethsemane. For Jesus it was a yielding to His *Father's* view of crucifixion. For you it will be the same.

> *I have a will; that will is opposed to Your will, Father. Tonight our wills move in opposite directions.*
>
> *It is I who yield. I place My opinion concerning this matter on the altar of sacrifice. Let the events continue.*
>
> *Let men do the will of God. Let Me be crucified.*

How do you feel about this immutable scene? Would you change it? Was there gain or loss from Christ's yielding?

As you ponder that question, recall to mind again who it is that authors all crucifixions! Including yours! Will there be gain or loss from *your* crucifixion? Gethsemane, or the lack of a Gethsemane, is the determining factor.

Crucifixion is viewed as an unprofitable catastrophe. Your Lord sees crucifixion as the central event of His life! He sees crucifixion as central in your life! To Him the cross is part of His work in your life. God's view of suffering is the reversal of all that mortals understand.

You see crucifixion as gore. He sees it as glory. The human mind simply cannot comprehend that. God the Father wanted His only begotten Son to be publicly, shamefully crucified. Today the Son does not hesitate to so arrange the circumstances of your life as to cause you to pass through this same experience.

As a Gethsemane awaited Him, so a Gethsemane most certainly awaits you.

Your Lord's Gethsemane was to yield to His Father. He found that very difficult to do, but he did; and as a result of that yielding he was nailed to a cross. Until He yielded, there could be no crucifixion. Once He yielded, events and circumstances became irreversible. Your Lord, in Gethsemane, had quite literally taken up His own cross.

Yielding allows crucifixion. Resistance nullifies it.

But I did not know these things when I was so brutally mistreated by Christians. I resisted; therefore, I had no Gethsemane. Today finds me angry. The memories are still vivid. The pain, the resentments, are still with me. I missed my Gethsemane!

Not necessarily. Gethsemane is not a place, nor is it a specific time.

For most believers Gethsemane must come *after* crucifixion. After all, Gethsemane is simply that hour when you finally align your will with the will of God. It is when you agree, accept, embrace...your crucifixion. Some, like the second thief, have to do that *after* the fact!!

The thief had to have his Gethsemane while nailed to a cross and breathing his last breath. So might you.

Most Christians are unfamiliar with the meaning of the cross as it has to do with the Christian life. In general, believers are unfamiliar with the vast destruction of a crucifixion. Consequently, Christians are utterly unprepared for the suffering involved.

Unprepared for the cross in their lives, they must discover its meaning, which requires that they have their Gethsemane *after* they encounter the cross. In the mercy of God, this is allowed.

Gethsemane is not a when or a where, but Gethsemane is a *must*. Without facing *your* Gethsemane, the crucifixion you have known will destroy you... with no hope of resurrection. Allowing a Gethsemane to come into your life changes all that.

Your Lord had an awful moment as He struggled to reconcile His will with His Father's will. Mark this: The cross made Gethsemane a necessity for Him. Likewise, in order for you to be crucified in the way that is proper for Christians to be crucified, you, too, must find your Gethsemane. Gethsemane is still a necessity! The cross and Gethsemane are inseparably linked.

Difficult to grasp, is it not, that such things as Calvary and Gethsemane are still a necessity in your day! Yet, the first time you ever heard the fundamental facts of your faith, you surely noticed the words, "We enter into the sufferings of Christ."

When is the correct time for you to face your Gethsemane? When you can call out to your Lord and say, "No man crucified me; it was You, my dear Lord, and You alone. It was sent into my life for edification. To *that* crucifixion I yield."

74

In that moment you have grasped the meaning of the cross in the life of a Christian.

When is your time for Gethsemane? The time for your Gethsemane is now!

Your Lord had *His* Gethsemane *before* He was crucified. The believer, of more frail material, almost inevitably must have his Gethsemane of surrender during or *after*. Whether it be before or after, it is always agony.

Come with me now to a garden.

18

Many have come to this garden.

Strange as it seems, even the second thief had to make his way to this place. True, Betard was hanging on a cross at the time of his Gethsemane. Regardless of the place, he had found it. That is what is important.

The choicest servants of God have all had to find their way to this garden.

The first person ever to visit Gethsemane was your Lord. Perhaps the most difficult thought to deal with in all the Lord's earthly life is to find that He did not want to be in Gethsemane. But it is even more shocking to understand why He did not want to come here. The reason is dumbfounding!

Jesus Christ and His Father were having a profound disagreement. Your Lord had a wholly different opinion from His Father's concerning whether or not He should go to the cross.

Did it ever occur to you that Jesus was in disagreement—even conflict—with His Father? Like you, your Lord had difficulty facing a crucifixion. It was the only moment in all eternal history that the Father and Son had differing opinions. It happened once, and only once. In a garden. The issue...

Crucifixion at the hands of His own brethren!

The issue between the Father and Son was concerning an unjust crucifixion. Your Lord was having a difficult time facing into a Golgotha.

True, this conflict of wills between the Father and the Son did not cause Jesus to take matters into His own hands; nonetheless, there is no question: He did not want to be crucified.

The cross is a concept originating with the Father.

The Father, looking down the corridors of time, knew it would be difficult for you to deal with the cross.

Unbelievable, is it not, that the Father of your Lord wanted Jesus to be crucified?

Crucifixion is not a human value, it is a divine value. Within the human frame crucifixion is not something which can be willingly embraced. In every way crucifixion is a divine thing, outside the scope of man.

No wonder there was a Gethsemane! That place is a necessity, for any human daring to follow a divine path *will* come upon a Gethsemane. Each will tarry there until he realigns his will with divinity, or he will completely miss the divine way of things.

That garden is the place where frail humanity finally comes to agree with divinity; it is where you come, at last, to agree with your Father, with His will. You agree to be crucified. You yield even when everything in you shrinks back in horror. While there, you might be comforted in remembering this: You will never be closer to the human side of your Lord than in Gethsemane.

You must not continue in rejecting crucifixion. Somewhere...before...during...or after that nightmare, you must agree to be crucified. Agree to that which repels you, to that which you fear, to that which is horrible, ignominious and repulsive. Agree to take into your person that which was meant to destroy you. Agree to something which, in every way, seems so terribly unchristian!

Acquiesce to destruction. *That* is Gethsemane.

19

You must seek out and find...Gethsemane. The garden awaits all pilgrims. When you finally come there, you will find your Father is also there.

Even now He awaits you.

As you pass through its gates, pause and realize there is something beautiful and comforting here, in knowing your Lord also had great difficulty walking through these same gates. The fact that everything in Him was repelled at the thought of being crucified gives *you* permission to have a very difficult time accepting crucifixion. That fact gives you the right to struggle, to resist, to find it virtually impossible to agree to God's will. Your Lord's struggle with this same issue gives you the right to stand in awe, terror and confusion at divine values. It gives you permission to want to run, to hide, and to cry out, "No, Lord, this is more than I can handle. This time I cannot go along with You."

You now have permission from the highest possible source to *not* wish to be crucified by others. Especially when it is by your own brothers.

When a Christian is mistreated by another Christian, the outcome is very predictable. The offended Christian reacts negatively, sometimes vehemently, even viciously. True, your Lord did not act this way, but He did *hesitate*. Reread the story. Jesus Christ was against being crucified. When it comes to dealing with a crucifixion, when it comes to being nailed to a cross, all believers stand on similar ground. Hesitation is acceptable. But to reject?! Ah! This you must not do. You will lose something valuable if you do. Find comfort in the face of the reality of His struggle, but you must find no excuses.

Be comforted by this: Your Lord dreaded, even feared, crucifixion. There is even the possibility that He might have considered rejecting it. At the very least, He had a strong opinion in the matter. Your Lord had a will of His own. That will came into full view in Gethsemane. It was His first time ever to exercise His own will in the face of His Father's will. If *His* humanity was showing, then know that Golgotha has a way of bringing out everyone's humanity.

Is this not the most poignant and arresting scene? The will of Jesus the Carpenter pitted against the will of God His Father? Hear your own voice join His, "Let us not have me to be crucified."

No one has ever easily agreed to being nailed to lumber.

Difficult, yes. But to yield... this is the way, the only way, of all who follow Him. Listen to no other voice, nor logic, nor reason.

You now have permission—from high sources—to not desire to be crucified. You are not expected to look like the magnificent Christian in such an hour. But you are expected to deal with this act of ignominy. Gethsemane requires that you face your Lord, acknowledge this brutalizing experience as being God, and yield.

You have permission to feel the pain and fear. But you have the example of your Lord...to yield! To yield to all that which is contrary to you. It is your Lord's nature to yield to His Father. He won that yieldedness and brought it into the very fabric and nature of His being, in Gethsemane. You cannot do this, but He can—it is His nature to yield to the cross—and He dwells in you.

Oh, and beyond that, He is one with you. Yield to His yieldedness. Allow divine life, of which you are now a partaker, to swallow up human life.

He can do Gethsemane again! In you!

Turn this scene around. See it from the other side. Step into heavenly territory. There you see things beyond your comprehension. Look at this scene from the Father's view. You are confronted by values so foreign you cannot take them in.

Behold crucifixion through the eyes of God. Whether it be His only begotten Son... or you... God favors crucifixion!

The Father wanted His Son crucified!

It was also His will that you be crucified.

20

Just why did God allow this terrible ordeal in your life? Let us face that question full on.

Dare we now face the fact that He not only allowed it, but desired it? The answer lies in discovering the deepest mystery of the cross...the deepest secret of God as concerns *why* Jesus was crucified!

You are aware that He died on the cross to save men from their sins. But there is a personal matter here. The Father allowed crucifixion to come into the life of His Son for a very amazing reason.

Jesus Christ was crucified because there was something lacking in Him!

What??

There was something Jesus Christ did not know, which He needed to learn.

There was a lack in the life of Jesus Christ. The Word of God testifies to this startling statement.

What could Jesus, the Christ, the eternal Son, possibly lack? There were things Jesus Christ did not know and could not know, except He be crucified. The Father willed that Jesus Christ be crucified because Jesus Christ *needed* to be crucified to learn of these things.

Staggering, is it not? Nonetheless, Holy Scripture is clear.

> Although He was a Son,
> He *learned* obedience
> from the things He suffered.
>
> Hebrews 5:8

Jesus Christ learned something only a crucifixion could teach Him.

The Son *learned* to obey His Father, even when that included dying. Only a crucifixion could provide that classroom. He learned an obedience He had never known before.

This is not the kind of obedience which is simply obeying orders. This is obedience of a far higher, rarer kind. Here is obedience that speaks of full concert between Father and Son. This is a matter of *all things* being wrapped in yieldedness.

What profoundness there must be in such unique yieldedness. It means that whatever comes, however bad circumstances get, you are in a state of yieldedness. You do not need glory days. The good days and the bad days are the same because you abide in a state of yieldedness. All days, regardless of content, are *best* days.

Such was the Father's purpose in the Son.

But was that not already the constant state of the Son?

Yes, definitely. Until Gethsemane. Right up to the time of crucifixion. In all things...*except* being crucified. He had to learn to obey His Father when it came to this infamy.

The Father decreed that the Son *learn* to yield even to this.

So also is it with you!!

A crucifixion, and only a crucifixion, marked the discovery that, for a moment, there were limits to the Son's yieldedness.

Is it no wonder, then, that *you* have had a difficult time yielding to a crucifixion?

Two wills were in total concert. For a moment those two wills disagreed. Once that disagreement was settled, their wills became eternally one. Indistinguishably. Utterly. *One*. The center of that disagreement was a bloody cross; the disagreement was settled in a garden.

It is here, then, that you see obedience—obedience carried out in order to *learn*! To learn what? To learn to agree to being crucified.

In your case, it is to learn to be crucified even by other Christians.

When you have yielded your will to the worst thing that can happen, there is nothing larger out there! There just is not anything waiting out there to destroy you that is greater than a bloody, unfair crucifixion.

Thus, we see Gethsemane in its true light.

In that dark place, agree to the choreography, agree to the bystanders caught up in this drama, agree to your friends having forsaken you, agree to the blood and the gore, agree to the hammer and the nails and the wood, agree to the infamy, to the shame, the treachery, agree to the loss of your reputation for the rest of your life. Agree to lies and rumors which will never die. Agree to Caiaphas and Ananias. Agree to the worst and darkest and ugliest moments life can contain.

If you refuse your Gethsemane? You refuse only by persisting in believing your crucifixion to be something unjust and meted out by cruel men. This is not a healthy way to live. Take that road and what does your future hold? Perhaps it contains something you have never considered. Life may end up with a view of daily events being seen somewhat like this: "Ugly, vicious Christians, who do not have any decency about them, mistreated me. You do not know what they did to me. Give me a lemon; I am going to suck on it the rest of my life."

Such a life view may continue pouring forth from you from now on when *another* Christian mistreats you. It may spread until every instant of life is colored by such a view. Refuse healing now, and a simple scratch may do you in.

> *Lord, I yield. In your eyes my crucifixion was*
> *something beautiful. It was your best for me.*
> *It was best for your purposes.*

May your Lord open your eyes to see there is purpose and beauty in that awful day when you were crucified by Christians.

If you yield, what of your future days?

21

Only a few hours before Jesus rose from the grave, men had been brutalizing Him. In that brutality of the cross Jesus had suffered the utter ends of pain.

Then He rose from the dead!

Quite a turnaround!

What happened next?

Remember how resentful He was? The anger He displayed? Remember how He stepped out of the tomb vowing vengeance? Remember, even as He rose He spat on the ground and cursed Caiaphas and Ananias? Do you recall how He swore revenge on all His tormentors and placed curses on all those who crucified Him?

Recall how—when He gathered His disciples—that He recounted every detail of His trial, every lie, every false testimony? Remember how full of bitterness His words? How He could not stop talking about what they had done to Him?

Do you remember these words:

"Then there was the time when one of them claimed that I said I would destroy Herod's Temple... well, that is not true...they twisted My words...I never said that. And can you believe the rumors about Me!"

Remember how He recounted the way the bodyguard of the high priest slapped Him in the face? How He caustically denounced the false witnesses? Remember when He told about the pitiful living condition of the prison? Remember His voice cracking as He pointed out that He would be disfigured throughout all eternity because of the scars on His body: "Now I have to live with these grotesque scars in My hands and feet. And every time I see them it will remind Me of their evil. I will never forgive them."

Did you notice that in virtually every conversation He had after His resurrection, He referred back to the way He had been mistreated at Golgotha? Did you notice the dark resentment, the worm of bitterness that ate into His soul?

You don't remember such things??

But you have noticed such talk from fellow Christians who have been crucified by fellow believers, have you not?

Here is the hallmark of the resurrection of your Lord: Having arisen from the grave, He never once referred to the events of His crucifixion.

Not once.

Not even one word.

Such is the hallmark of all true resurrections! The past is forever gone! *Resurrection* is beyond that which is dead.

Resurrection means to arise from out of death into a new realm, a new time continuum where *the past never happened*.

Proof of a real Gethsemane, proof of a crucifixion meted out to you by the hate of Christians, yet surrendered by you into the hand of God...that proof is found in the attitude of Jesus Christ when He rose.

May you find that same grace.

Resurrection is a demarcation. Everything before resurrection no longer exists. It never happened!!

That is the essence of resurrection. Everything before never happened. Everything after resurrection is new and has no connection with events of the past! After the resurrection, all things belong to a new creation. That new creation has no relationship with anything which had gone before it.

A creation so new, and an old creation so annihilated, that you cannot remember!

What an *honor* to be crucified! Why? Because beyond crucifixion is resurrection...and that new creation. All the past evaporated. It is *gone*. It never existed!

The past no longer exists! The past is not just ignored or forgotten. It never happened!

That is resurrection.

But...

22

Resurrection comes only because there is first a crucifixion. The cross *must* always predicate resurrection. The second is impossible without the first.

Can a pilgrim learn a greater lesson than this: Crucifixion is God's invitation to resurrection.

When one desires resurrection, he is also requesting the cross.

If your Lord decreed a crucifixion in your life, it was an invitation to know resurrection. That invitation, dear child of God, is an honor.

The essence of crucifixion is that it is a portal to pass through to come into the fullness of resurrection.

Crucifixion is an invitation of the highest order to the highest of realms.

A crucified one has within his grasp the highest plane of Christian living—life *beyond* crucifixion. Living in resurrection. That is the highest order of Christian living.

The goal of your Lord in all crucifixions is to bring a person to a place of living which is beyond this visible creation—living in a new creation where the past has evaporated into nothingness!

Jesus Christ lost everything in crucifixion. Everything He accomplished on this earth was destroyed. When men laid Him in a grave, there was nothing He could show for His thirty-three years on earth.

Yet, in all this loss of all things, He endured the cross, despised the shame. Why? Because He knew there was glory out there in the future. That is how it works with crucifixion.

Right now you may be hanging on a cross, but it has purpose. There is a resurrection awaiting you, one so glorious it will obliterate the very memory of that cross.

See the beauty, see the honor, in having been crucified by Christians. God's purpose? That purpose includes your resurrection.

Resurrection living is higher than the life previously lived! Always.

Thank Him for the privilege of being crucified. See the sheer joy, the unparalleled opportunity which *only* crucifixion affords you. See before you a blinding light. It is a new day. Behold that new creation. That new creation, lived only in resurrection, lies far beyond and far above the point where crucifixion can reach you.

Resurrection is at your fingertips. But as surely as there can be no resurrection without crucifixion, there can be no *true* crucifixion without Gethsemane. Make your peace with God.

He wanted your crucifixion so you might see your own reaction; that you might view your dark side; that your dark side, so much a part of your life and personality, would be dealt with; that you might find your way to His sovereign hand and yield to the mysteries of His ways; and that you might place your will in concert with His.

Join your Lord in Gethsemane, join Him at Golgotha. *Then* can you join Him in resurrection!

He wants you to allow Him to be your all. He desired that you would come to accept *all things* as originating from Him. In love!

At this moment your Lord walks and lives in resurrection! He lives *beyond*. He lives beyond the worst that can happen. He lives beyond the worst that can happen because the very worst happened to Him. He lives *beyond* Death!

Such a path of glory is now open to you. A resurrected Lord awaits a dying believer.

What is the difference between life and *resurrected* life? This: You can kill life! Look at Golgotha and learn that even divine life could be killed. You cannot kill resurrection life. You cannot kill divine life which has passed through death. You cannot kill divine life that is on the other side of crucifixion. Divine life...crucified. Divine life...dead. Divine life...passed through death. Divine life...*resurrected*. There is nothing that can touch *that* life. When you have risen from the dead, *nothing* can touch you!!

There is a great and glorious purpose in the cross, is there not?

23

What if, in the future, you are once again brutally treated by Christians? The thought is abhorrent, is it not? But it has happened. There *are* Christians who have been coldly, calculatingly crucified by others...more than once.

What would be your lot if that happened again?

If you have dealt with that first crucifixion, if you have forgiven your executors, if you have taken that first crucifixion as from the hand of God, *if you have risen from the dead*...then, if it happened again, you will once again survive. You will serve Him again...freely, trustingly.

By the grace that could only be given by the Holy Spirit, and by gifts that are not man's to give, you dealt with your Lord; and He dealt with you, touched you, and gave you the grace to live. He will do so *again*.

You will come out of that trauma, rising again, ready to risk all, all over again! For His glory. And His honor.

It is difficult to be destroyed by that which has already been conquered. Men are rarely ruined by what could not previously ruin them.

But if that first sordid mess is not dealt with, if you never break free of the memories, if there is no Gethsemane, then that second crucifixion will only drive you deeper into a hopeless chasm of bitterness. That second crucifixion, in fact, will be no crucifixion at all. It will be nothing more than another ugly scene: Christians fighting with Christians. You will but view it as further proof of how vicious God's people are. It will but add to your nightmarish memories—memories like unto the ones which even now haunt the corridors of your mind.

Is this the lot you wish to choose for yourself? Worse, is this a picture of your future? If for no other reason but to continue in a childlike love of Jesus, choose crucifixion... at the hand of God.

Let us say you deal with being crucified by Christians on so exalted a plane, what lies ahead?

24

A life higher than the life of God?

The very idea is incomprehensible. Everyone knows that the life of God is the highest life of all.

But it is not.

The highest life in all universal history is God's life...passed through death. God's life...resurrected. *That* is the highest life.

The Lord's greatest enemy, His last enemy, His *only* enemy, was Death. When one has defeated his greatest enemy, there is no other enemy. A lesser enemy than your greatest enemy can never inflict on you a pain greater than that which your greatest opponent can inflict. The defeat of your greatest enemy places the remaining enemies in a far weaker position.

When you have been hit by the worst possible circumstances and you rise in victory from out of the ashes, those former circumstances have lost their cutting edge. Their power is broken.

Nothing can stop Jesus Christ because He has ascended over Death. All other enemies have less to throw against Him than did Death. There is no other enemy who is as great as Death. Jesus Christ was slain by Death, then slew Death and rose again. Death cannot ever again touch Him. Death is less than what Christ is. Also, crucifixion is less than what Christ is.

What does this mean to you? This triumphant Lord, and His triumphant life form, lives in you! Let *that* life live. Let that life lead you to your death. Allow that life to raise you out of the gore, pain, destruction and ashes of Golgotha and death. Embrace the demands forced on you by crucifixion. Until someone comes up with something to place in your life which is worse than being crucified by Christians, then being crucified by Christians is less than the life operating in you.

Do you realize what this means to your Christian life? You are able to go forth in your walk with the Lord, higher up and further in, until a day you are hit by something worse than being crucified.

Is not crucifixion, then, of great value? Can you not see the fingerprints of God on your present situation? Your Lord has made available to you the possibility of living above the cruelty of men (even the cruelty of Christians), unscarred!

Settle your crucifixion. Resurrection awaits. It will take an act greater than crucifixion to inhibit your upward walk with Him. Such prospects are unlikely!

Your Lord believes you have a right to live by resurrection life. Resurrection life is a life that exists only as it is life that has fully walked through the valley of crucifixion.

He awaits your permission, permission to be crucified in the manner and style of Christ. *That* gives Him permission to raise you from the grave.

(Kicking and screaming, resenting and reasoning, and short cuts, are not part of *His* ways. You never get to create *your* version of how you are to be crucified. You submit to that which is thrust upon you.)

Still, there is more.

25

In Which Creation Do You Now Live?

The cross stands between two creations, the dividing mark between two realms, two universes, between an ancient creation and a new one. That new creation is Christ Himself.

One creation is fallen...and terribly old. This creation exists up to the time of the cross, but never exists beyond the cross.

That second creation, that new realm, that entirely new creation, lives only *beyond* the cross.

The new creation is quite remarkable. It knows nothing of the old creation! Nor does the new creation know anything of the unfairness of a cross. The history of the first creation ends by telling the story of the cross. That is Volume One. Volume Two is the history of the new creation. That history begins with the story of an empty tomb. It knows no previous history. History, for the new creation, is the story of the birth of that creation at the time Christ resurrected! This volume contains no records of anything which existed previous to the resurrection; it has no knowledge of any creation which existed before it came into being. It has no memory of evil deeds. That unique creation draws its very being, its life, its sustenance from the highest Life there is...the divine, resurrected Life of God. Your Lord is the only Life in this wondrous new creation.

Do you recall the relationship you had with Christ the first few days after you were saved—believing all things, trusting all things, hoping all things and rejoicing in *all* things.

Allowing the old creation you are now living in to disappear forever, the beauty of resurrection awaits. Walking into that new creation, you discover that the things in the old creation no longer exist.

Is not acceptance of the cross a small thing, then?

The hour is late. We have spoken together long enough. I would close our time together by asking a question of two people who have been crucified by Christians. One of these two people is *you*. The other is not you, and never will be.

26

A Closing Question

Which of these two people is you? The answer
reveals itself. How so? The answer you give allows you
to discover which creation you live in. Here is the
question. There can be only two possible responses.
Which response you give decides *who* you are.

Have you ever been crucified by Christians?

One Possible Response

Yes, I was crucified by Christians.

It happened to me unexpectedly! I was not conform-
ing, so someone corrected me. Later I was confronted.
Eventually rumors about me were flying everywhere.
Finally, I was severely warned. By that time just about
everyone had turned against me. I received harsh,
questioning letters and phone calls. New rumors came to

me daily. Soon just about everyone I knew who was a Christian had turned from me or had been turned against me. Many viciously attacked me. I never heard so many lies and distortions. Finally, I was excommunicated, reviled, sworn at. My life was virtually ruined.

I confess that even now I find it hard to forget the unjust way I was treated. The words still ring in my ears. Everything in my innards burns as I remember all those cruelties. I will never be able to trust Christians again. Surely, I will never trust a Christian leader again.

Sometimes I find that, even when casually talking with others, the thoughts and memories seep into my words.

I confess that I am still a bit skeptical—sometimes even critical—of most everything I hear that is going on among Christians.

As to my spiritual life? My walk with Christ? Well, it is pretty much on hold. Nothing much has moved since that experience.

I understand you are about to speak with another believer who was crucified by Christians. I hope his lot is better than mine. Maybe he is handling it better than I am. On the other hand, I doubt that he—or anyone else— has ever been treated quite as unchristian as I have been.

A Second Possible Response

Have I ever been crucified by Christians? I am not sure.

You heard that I had been? Cruelly? Unjustly?

106

Strange, I do not recall.

Perhaps it did happen. Or did it? I am not at all sure. Mistreated by other believers? No, I really cannot remember.

Oh, perhaps such a thing may have occurred in some other creation, and in some other time continuum, but I do not know. All things which come into my life are from the hand of my Lord. I am sure that whatever has befallen me originated in His heart, and in love.

He is the Triumphant One. In Him, at least here in this realm, all things are

of Him
> *by* Him
>> *for* Him
>>> *to* Him
>>>> *through* Him
>>>> and *in Him!*

Memories of all else seem to have fled away. In Him I live in light. In Him I walk in ascended life.

Have you ever been
crucified
by
Christians?

THE CHOICE IS YOURS.

27

As we come to our final moments together, may I add a closing word? This planet is in desperate need of men and women who have been crucified.

How desperate is the need of men and women whom the Lord is allowing to be crucified. They, in turn, need to *meet* men and women who have been crucified. Men and women who have not only been crucified, but who have yielded to it, saved themselves from nothing in it, and yielded to the hand of God. Resurrected believers! Resurrected from crucifixion! There are few Christians today—or in any age—who understand *anything* about the cross. There has never been a generation which has had enough believers who have truly known the cross.

The Christian world remains almost void of broken men and women. Counterwise, brokenness is often looked upon more as a matter to flee from than to embrace. Being tough and *un*broken is envied and applauded. Escaping the harsher aspects of the cross is practiced daily.

Needed: men and women who are *present* at the scene when the Lord is working brokenness in the lives of His other children. Needed: unblemished testimonies of those who yielded fully to the fullness of the cross. Needed: children of Golgotha and Joseph's tomb.

God knows how desperately are needed crucified, resurrected Christians.

Why did God allow this tragedy into your life? Perhaps the reason, or reasons, are clearer now.

Now add this one: Perhaps your Lord also desired a crucifixion to come to you so that *you* might be one of those on the scene with *your* life, your testimony, your experience, of being crucified... to comfort, to aid, to guide, to encourage another gaunt believer who is being mercilessly crucified by others.

There was a man named Paul who had been defamed and crucified by his own people, beaten and crucified by the secular world, betrayed and crucified by professing believers. His work was nearly destroyed even by men who professed to be fellow Christian workers.

Paul took it all from the hand of God, ran from none of it, altered none of it, yielded to all of it, and walked on!

That man comforted, aided, and quite literally saved the lives of innumerable believers in his lifetime. Then, down through history, his words and testimony have comforted and healed millions. This all came about because he triumphed in crucifixion and rose from the bludgeoning of its death.

Notice that as an outcome of his terrible ordeals, the man did not forsake presenting the cross to others. He joyed in presenting the cross to others. He even went out of his way to exalt the need of the cross in the life of all believers.

Proclaiming that cross, he founded churches. Proclaiming that cross he saved those churches from destruction. Men and women followed his example, responded to his testimony, and in dying, lived! So, also, did the churches.

Paul was living proof you can come out of innuendos, lies, attacks, false reports, beatings, plots, setbacks, failures and even the destruction of your work, *and still rise from the grave*... and from there, point others to Christ, joyfully. Paul embraced unjust sufferings, reveled in a cross and gloried in a crucifixion that both killed him and gave him life. He revealed a cross that had killed his Lord and had given Him life, then proclaimed that all believers were to expect to enter into that same experience.

That servant of Christ, because he willingly yielded to *a large* number of unjust, cruel, heartless crucifixions, has been an abundant field of life to millions.

So, also, Peter. So, also, John.

So, also, your Lord.

So, also, other men and women sprinkled out among the pages of church history.

At this very moment there are Christians all over this planet being crucified. Who will reach out to them, and show them Christ?

111

At secular employment, at the cruel hands of bosses who are above them, or peers beside them, of employees below them... right now there are men and women who suddenly—without warning—are being fired and cast into the terror of unexpected unemployment. Right now there are ministers being persecuted by churches, and churches being persecuted by ministers. The iconoclast in parachurch organizations, mission boards (and other assorted religious organizations) are being treated unbelievably cruelly by peers. Men and women *inside* the traditional church are being flayed. Men and women *outside* the organized church are being vehemently, mercilessly slandered.

Where is the pathfinder? Where is that one who has already been there? Where is the voice of comfort? Where is the man who has already drunk the cup? Where is the woman who has tread the winepress? Where is the layman who has drowned in deep waters, the minister who has scars that are healed? Where are those who call to the suffering one, "This is your finest hour, take it at its highest!" Where is the voice that cries, "Here is true honor. Allow this crucifixion, that you might live again!"

Where are the resurrected ones?

Where is the heart that testifies, "It is of God. Continue. Further in! Higher up."

Where is the cross?

Oh, dear one, invite the nails!!

Adieu

Our time must come to an end.

You have spoken so articulately about Christians and their relationship to the cross. Are you not one who also has experienced crucifixion?

To answer your question is to bring to light one final matter, that of your relationship to those who so terribly mistreated you.

To answer your question, no, I am not one who has been crucified. I am one of those who participated in crucifying the Christ. I am that soldier who drove the spear into His side!

Remember that your Lord calls on you to forgive those who acted so wrongfully toward you. He is sovereign, and His history with such people does not end when they crucified you. Perhaps one day they will join in knowing the kind of fate which befell you.

Forgive those who crucified you. In so doing, receive forgiveness.

Let us now say adieu. The future is yours to choose.

The curtain has closed. Our two players have slipped from the stage. In a moment the theatre's doors will once more be closed, the lights extinguished. It is time, too, for us to go.

If you do not mind, let us say a very brief good-bye now, as I feel the need to spend some time alone. Perhaps you are of the same mind.

SeedSowers

COMFORT AND HEALING

A Tale of Three Kings *(Edwards)*.. 8.95
The Prisoner in the Third Cell *(Edwards)*................................. 7.95
Letters to a Devastated Christian *(Edwards)*............................ 5.95
Healing for those who have been Crucified by Christians *(Edwards)*.......8.95
Dear Lillian *(Edwards)*..5.95

OTHER BOOKS ON CHURCH LIFE

Climb the Highest Mountain *(Edwards)*...................................9.95
The Torch of the Testimony *(Kennedy)*..................................14.95
The Passing of the Torch *(Chen)*...9.95
Going to Church in the First Century *(Banks)*..........................5.95
When the Church was Young *(Loosley)*..................................14.95
Church Unity *(Litzman, Nee, Edwards)*...................................14.95
Let's Return to Christian Unity *(Kurosaki)*...............................14.95

CHRISTIAN LIVING

Final Steps in Christian Maturity *(Guyon)*.............................12.95
The Key to Triumphant Living *(Taylor)*.................................. 9.95
Turkeys and Eagles *(Lord)*... 8.95
Beholding and Becoming *(Coulter)*....................................... 8.95
Life's Ultimate Privilege *(Fromke)*.. 7.00
Unto Full Stature *(Fromke)*.. 7.00
All and Only *(Kilpatrick)*... 7.95
Adoration *(Kilpatrick)* 8.95
Release of the Spirit *(Nee)* 5.00
Bone of His Bone *(Huegel)* 8.95
Christ as All in All *(Haller)* 9.95

Please write or call for our current catalog:

SeedSowers
P.O. Box 285
Sargent, GA 30275

800-228-2665
www.seedsowers.com